Better Homes and Gardens®
studio spaces

Better Homes and Gardens®

studio spaces

projects,
inspiration &
ideas for your
creative place

WILEY

John Wiley & Sons, Inc.

24 EASY PROJECTS

contents

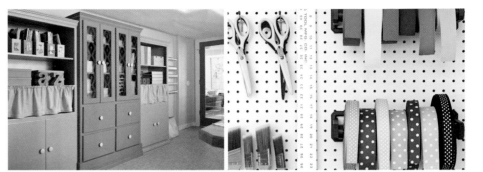

3» Get Organized

5» Shared Spaces

4» Small Spaces

6» Project Ideas

Free yourself to pursue your creative endeavors by designing a studio that fits your personality and your organizational needs. You'll enjoy the process and the results all the more.

it's
personal

What kind of space do you need to call your own? Are you an artist who needs an entire room, that's both inspiring and a retreat, to devote to your craft? Maybe you and your spouse need a space that suits both of your needs. Or perhaps you have only a corner of the family room to spare, and somehow you need it to be both family-friendly yet functional for a variety of tasks, such as gift-wrapping, scrapbooking, and computing.

If you're the creative type, and you can relate to any of the described scenarios, get ready to be inspired to design the space of your dreams. Inside, you'll find a collection of the most beautiful studios ever assembled in one book. Get a glimpse inside some of the most fabulous spaces belonging to fabric artists, scrapbookers, and paper crafters, whose studios are truly a reflection of their personalities and their art. Be amazed by the transformations of dark, cluttered, unorganized spaces into stunning, organized, and inspiring studios. Plus, learn the tips and tricks of several studios that serve multiple purposes: playroom, home office, and even guest bedroom. And throughout it all, there are plenty of ideas that you can adapt for organizing all your tools, embellishments, fabrics, and more, along with step-by-step projects that you can use for personalizing the room.

As you browse through this book, be sure to take note of any ideas that might work in designing your own studio. Near the back of the book, you'll find the "Workbook"—graph paper that we hope you'll find useful for planning the layout of your own space.

But most importantly, remember that a studio is a highly personal space. Whatever the size or function, there isn't a one-size-fits-all solution. Our hope is that you'll use the ideas inside this book to find your own inspiration for creating a space that functions well, inspires you, and keeps you creating.

1

Designer Studios

Get a glimpse into the places where some of the most talented quilters, fabric artists, and scrapbookers create, and find out what inspires them.

A PLACE FOR everything

Take the advice of a seasoned scrapper—make your storage options as pretty as they are practical.

Written by DEBRA WITTRUP   Photographed by TATJANA ALVEGARD   Produced by JENNIFER KELTNER

Vicki Boutin

Designer and scrapbooker Vicki Boutin is a pro at repurposing things and rethinking the obvious. For example, her new house plan said "dining room," but Vicki had other ideas for the 11×14" space. "When we were building the house, I knew that a dining room wouldn't get used," she says. "Instead, I wanted it for my scrap room because my other favorite place to be is in the

The consistency of Vicki's color palette makes a busy room full of supplies remarkably attractive and inviting. "I like my work spaces to be practical yet full of flash and flair," she says. Shelving and a china hutch from IKEA fulfill her practical needs, while a bargain chandelier of plastic and glass adds the flair.

adjoining kitchen. I can be active with the rest of my family while I am creating."

Vicki's decision to stick to a color palette of black, white, and red guided her choices from the start. "Knowing my color scheme allowed me to shop with confidence," Vicki says. To keep things affordable, Vicki shopped discount stores and flea markets and even did a bit of searching in her own home, looking for underused furniture.

After much mixing and matching, the result is surprisingly coherent. White, black, and natural shelves and cabinets line the walls, while a substantial black work table anchors the center of the room. Dozens of containers holding Vicki's scrapping supplies fill the shelves. And never mind its original purpose—if Vicki

can find a use for a container, she buys it.

To maintain order, Vicki stores like items together. Paper goes in vertical boxes, stickers in a basket, buttons and ribbon in jars, and embellishments in boxes. And while everything has its place, she still gets to experience the thrill of the hunt. "The space is like my own little scrap boutique," she says.

Turn the page to see more of Vicki's storage ideas, as well as a peek at an extra basement scrap space that lets her spend time with her family while she's scrapbooking.

An inexpensive curtain rod with clip rings displays favorite pages—an idea Vicki borrowed from a friend. "I like to see my creations rather than just put them in albums," Vicki says. "I use my pages as artwork throughout the house."

A graduated corner shelf taken from the former nursery adds a curvaceous element to the angular furnishings in the room and maximizes storage space.

An underused sofa console table gets a new lease on life in Vicki's scrap room. Part display piece and part organization system, the table provides a lot of storage in a small, shallow space. Vintage wire locker baskets chock-full of supplies line the bottom shelf, while a series of oval lined baskets keep more materials tucked away underneath.

An elegant tapered hand holds necklaces Vicki made. A pair of small decorative suitcases and several jars lend color and pattern, as well as storage options, in the background.

Vicki inherited this jewelry hanger from a friend. She uses it to display treasured photos on clips and to hang used crystals from an old lamp for a bit of bling. "I like the dangles," she says. "There's just no rhyme or reason for some of this stuff."

Vicki buys vintage metal flower frogs whenever she finds them. Besides supporting handmade cards for display, the frogs also are useful when photographing cards individually.

Someone else's trash became Vicki's treasure when her mother brought her this old dress form. "It still has a name written on it, but that just adds to the charm," Vicki says. She decked out the form in handmade jewelry and decorative pins.

Another chance find, this bookcase decorated with salvaged banister rails makes a great spot for larger tools and magazine boxes.

Vicki found this old wooden bobbin at a flea market. "Part of the fun is searching out these amazing pieces," she says. She uses it to display pretty ribbons from her collection. A decorative stickpin holds them in place.

"I'm always inspired by the materials that surround me," Vicki says. Rolls of vintage crepe paper in Vicki's favorite hues inject color and character into the room.

When she starts a new project, Vicki goes shopping in her boutique scrap room. "I usually take in an empty basket, look through the containers, and then start filling it up with the things I want to use," she says.

A two-tier kitchen fruit basket keeps stamps and embossing powders in view and easy to grab.

A magnetic board increases the wall's storage capacity, while a memo board allows Vicki to display finished pages and inspirational pieces. An old signage letter kicks in a bit of personality.

Bonus Room

In an effort to spend more time with her family while she's scrapping, Vicki found a corner wall in the basement and set up a small, efficient workstation. "The desk is large enough to spread things out and allows me to work in the family room when the kids are down here," Vicki says. "I can be productive and part of what's going on at the same time." A plain bookcase and rolling cart add storage nearby.

A wall-mounted kitchen organization system from IKEA transforms the wall above the desk into supply space.

A former microwave cart finds new purpose in the basement scrap corner. "With the right containers, I can fill the cart with supplies and still keep it looking tidy," Vicki says. "And having some storage on wheels is pretty handy, too."

Make It Yours
Vicki's advice for mixing storage containers

✳ **USE REPETITION**

Repeat shapes and sizes, use the same or similar color throughout a space, and gather multiple items from the same types of materials, such as metal, wicker, or glass.

✳ **INJECT COLOR**

Choose a color palette and stick to it as you find things for your room. Knowing your color scheme helps you make decisions as you shop. But don't be afraid to add an unexpected color here and there for visual interest.

✳ **MAKE IT PRETTY**

Look for pattern, elegance, and panache in your containers. Even workrooms can be beautiful.

✳ **ADD WHIMSY**

Seek out the unusual. Include repurposed things that reflect your interests and serve your storage needs.

✳ **TAKE YOUR TIME**

Build your container collection over time. Don't try to do it all at once. If you do find things that you love or that are at the right price, grab them!

✳ **HAVE FUN**

It's all about the joy of the hunt and the pleasure you find in your crafts.

✳ **CREATE YOUR BALANCE**

Move things around until they feel right. Symmetry is the easiest way to achieve balance, but it also can be found by weighting objects evenly in a space.

1. A lingerie drawer organizer stands in as a sorter of brads, pins, and other items stored by size. **2.** A vintage honey bucket holds ribbon and braid. **3.** Attesting to Vicki's fascination with dress forms, this wire earring hanger holds cards, tags, and occasionally an apron wrapped around its middle. **4.** Vicki loved this wire basket, but its original English rose accent didn't fit her decor. She bought it anyway and altered it with sheet-music paper and embellishments before filling it with scrap supplies. **5.** Proving Vicki's premise that even basic supply storage can be beautiful, this jar full of deliciously colorful buttons beckons the eye. **6.** One of Vicki's favorite times to shop for containers is during the spring when garden centers put out their new merchandise. Originally intended to be a portable herb garden, this wire basket now holds Vicki's collection of pens.

7. "I found this woven bag at a garage sale," Vicki says. "It was dirty and full of old tools—my mom thought it was the ugliest thing ever." Cleaned up and put into service, the bag holds a collection of stickers in style. **8.** Vintage muffin tins are handy when sorting things by color or type. They're also ideal for holding small items that might get lost in a larger container. **9.** This old lunch pail found new life on Vicki's china hutch as portable ink storage. **10.** An enamel bathroom organizer keeps small items corralled on the surface of the china hutch. "You can have tons of loose little bits in scrapbooking. It's easy to lose track of them if they're not visible," Vicki says.

Nashville-based textile designer and author Anna Maria Horner channels her playful spirit into bold fabric designs in her fun, vintage-inspired sewing studio.

fabric forward

With a bent toward vintage and vibrant, this artist's studio comes alive with fabric in every nook and cranny. Photographed by JAMES CARRIÉRE

Growing up surrounded by her father's paintings and her mother's handmade clothes, Anna Maria Horner dressed her Barbie dolls in outfits she fashioned from fabric scraps. That same artistic bent moved to fabric designs, paintings, and the clothing line she and her mother developed.

Today, Anna Maria finds herself at home inside her own sewing room, where she's surrounded by the saturated colors and organic shapes found on the fabrics that she knows so well. Here, her sewing station is backed with a cork wall filled with photographs, sketches, and fabric samples. Vintage candleholders are topped with playful pincushions in a mix of colorful fabrics. Along the adjoining wall, a cubby hutch

on top of a desk overflows with colorful stacks of fabrics, bins, and jars of tools. Underneath, a fabric panel hides unsightly clutter.

Anna Maria offers the following advice about creating your own workspace: "Fabrics are an inexpensive way to add style to any room," Anna Maria says. "Pull in pops of color and pattern one at a time with pillows, canvases, and curtains.

"Even if you don't sew, you can incorporate fabrics at home," she says. "Some fabrics can be simply stretched over a frame and hung as wall art. Or just cover a bulletin board with fabric."

Anna Maria Horner

A casual collection of Anna Maria's needlepoint pillows and hand-hooked rugs are propped up against a wall adorned with button cards and inspirational sketches.

Swatches from Anna Maria's fabric collections are draped over wooden dowels attached to the wall above her computer.

Anna Maria uses her fabrics to cover magazine holders. She makes her holders out of old FedEx boxes. To replicate the look, wrap and fold fabric around a box form and secure with either fabric glue or iron-on adhesive strips.

a fresh take
on the past

Amy Butler

Designer Amy Butler draws inspiration from vintage textiles to create her hip, stylish fabrics and patterns.

Written by ALLISON ENGEL   Photographed by PERRY STRUSE

I f there is such a thing as a charmed life, designer Amy Butler may be living it.

She works from her home in a small college town in Ohio. Woods provide natural beauty outside her windows, while inside she's surrounded by a vibrant mix of vintage fabrics, cool furniture, and sundry antique objects she finds amusing.

Her husband, David Butler, a skilled graphic artist who designs fashion-forward brand

Amy Butler's studio is a mix of salvage furniture finds and flea-market treasures.

development campaigns, also works from their home, in a studio next to Amy's. They share their creatively arranged rooms with four rescued cats and enjoy a wide circle of family and longtime friends who live nearby.

The allure of Amy's fabric designs is that they draw upon vintage textiles but look utterly fresh, thanks to stylized patterns and hip color combinations. A vaguely Pacific Rim print escapes looking touristy by being executed in brown, blue, avocado, and white. A rakish stripe includes lime green, cranberry, aqua, and tan. A paisley is reinterpreted in mod '60s colors.

Amy's passion for textiles, specifically vintage textiles, includes the joy of hunting for them.

"I've been collecting vintage pieces for 17 years," she says. "I started in college [because] I wanted to make my apartment beautiful, and buying older fabrics at flea markets was an affordable way to decorate my space.

"This is still in effect, as I continually purchase special pieces to make one-of-a-kind pillows or throws and deck my kitchen out in great old tablecloths or printed linen towels. I imagine I'll be collecting them for the rest of my days."

Julio, one of the Butlers' many cats, perches on a chair covered in Gracious Lotus from Amy's Sunbloom home decor collection.

Amy's bags, pillows, and quilt designs incorporate her love of vintage textiles, yet have a modern feel.

Amy uses a mix of paint chips and pictures for inspiration in designing.

> **Often I'm inspired
> to make something pretty
> for my home or for my friends.
> I just create things
> that I want to surround me.**
> —AMY BUTLER

Everything Old Is New Again

"Stylish, Unique, Charming & Fresh" is the tagline for Amy Butler's designs, and the same could be said for the designer herself. Amy grew up near Dayton, Ohio, and graduated from Columbus College of Art and Design, where she studied fashion and surface design. A longtime sewer, she has quilted in the past, but her current schedule doesn't allow her much time to sew.

Amy began creating bags because there were projects she wanted to give as gifts, but she was unable to find a pattern that suited her needs. She first sold her handmade designs while living in Kansas City in the late 1980s, selling passport-size bags to boutiques around the country. After moving back to Ohio in 1992, she and David began their Art of the Midwest design studio.

In addition to their designing, Amy and David always have enjoyed making the rounds of thrift stores and antique shops together, something they grew up doing since the parents of both were antiques collectors. A few years ago they distilled their decorating style into

Vintage pins are at the ready, artfully displayed on cake stands and in old dishes nestled among pincushions. Amy occasionally uses the pins on projects.

a book, *Found Style*. It describes a design sensibility that combines a turn-of-the-century Victorian mahogany settee with a midcentury modern coffee table and Bertoia chair.

Amy calls her home studio "my little design nest," and she's made it cozy with lots of what she calls "yummy stuff," including an old mailbox filled with ribbons and yarns and a Victorian curio cabinet overflowing with beads, buttons, trims, and vintage jewelry.

Her burgeoning stash of vintage fabrics grew so large that she recently pruned it severely. What remains is stored on stainless-steel bakers' carts that she and David found for $50 at a restaurant salvage store. A lot of their studio furnishings came from hospital and restaurant salvage firms, Amy says.

It's clear that Amy Butler is on to something. Working on projects she loves, surrounded by the people she loves, in the small town where she feels comfortable, she has created products—and a lifestyle—that are striking a chord everywhere.

Amy pins small totems, photographs, and fabric swatches to her studio wall for design inspiration.

An odd-shaped attic and a case of plastic-phobia made storage a challenge when Erikia planned her scrapbook workplace.

VINTAGE VIBE

Erikia Ghumm

Erikia's keen eye for vintage finds and a homespun sense of style turned this challenging spot into her favorite room in the house. Written by JENNIFER WILSON Photographed by POVY KENDAL ATCHISON

When she bought her suburban Denver home seven years ago, scrapbook designer Erikia Ghumm's attic was, well, ugly.

Cheap white carpeting. Dark paneling. Low ceilings. Short walls. You get the picture.

Yet Erikia took a deep breath, rolled up her sleeves, and moved in anyway. "I just kind of put my stuff in there," she says. "Then I had to devise inexpensive storage to fit under the eaves.

And standard storage just wouldn't do.

"I don't like plastic, so it's difficult to find something that looks good," she says. "I didn't have much to spend, so I got creative."

Erikia rustled up bins and boxes from secondhand stores, estate sales, antiques shops, and friends. Old fruit and soda crates organize paints and albums, while colored boxes store old family photographs by date.

She fills suitcases with embellishments. Cookie tins and canning jars—sometimes found curbside—contain inks, embellishments, and flowers.

A few splurges bring the room together. Erikia saved and bought the colorful locker bins that line the bookshelf two at a time over the course of a year. "They were pricey,

but nothing else was sturdy enough," she says.

Old furniture—including a sofa and coffee table from her grandmother and chandeliers given by friends that Erikia embellished herself—lend the room a comfy, well-worn vibe. Erikia and her mother even sewed the curtains from thrift-store and vintage fabrics purchased online. The result is a place where she and her husband, Brian, gravitate to work on hobbies rather than watch television.

"This room totally fits me," she says. "It's a little vintage, a little artsy, and a comfortable place to work and hang out."

She personalizes her storage solutions with her creations, such as the tags on this wooden crate.

Erikia "beat up" this collection of storage cubes with alcohol ink and then replaced contemporary hardware with glass knobs.

From her kitschy snow-globe collection to the state plates on display, Erikia Ghumm's scrapbooking room fondly recalls another era. "I've always loved old things, ever since I was little," Erikia says.

Rather than having a mess of paint bottles cluttering her workspace, Erikia turned the supplies into tidy dots of color in vintage soda boxes. She groups them by hue to make them easier to locate—and nicer to look at. "It's less busy this way," she says.

Colorful locker bins hide "messy" items, such as accents, books, and cardmaking supplies. Below the bins, photo boxes hold old family pictures and negatives.

Make It Yours

Follow Erikia's lead to find unique storage solutions to fit a vintage style.

① SAVE A SPOT
Erikia heads to the couch when she wants to dream up a sketch.

② CORRAL EMBELLISHMENTS
Small items like eyelets and brads are easily retrievable in tiny jars housed inside square tins.

③ BREAK UP THE CLUTTER
Store buttons and stamps in old cookie tins piled on a vintage cake stand for convenience and style.

④ STACK IT UP
Old suitcases with "luggage tag" labels stash everything from photos to beads stacked in boxes.

⑤ CONCEAL IT
Old fruit crates found at an antiques store hide rubber stamps from view.

⑥ RESCUE AND REUSE
Erikia purchases bags of trinkets from Goodwill and scans garage sales for discarded treasures to decorate her home and crafts projects.

⑦ COVER IT UP
A spray-painted curtain rod covered in colorful vintage fabrics hides plastic drawers from view.

⑧ REUSE FINDS
Old cans and crates become perfect storage for tools.

dream
DESIGN

Longing for a sewing retreat? Heed the tips from this popular quilt designer to create a serene space that you can escape to anytime. Written by JUDITH STERN FRIEDMAN   Photographed by ADAM ALBRIGHT

Jean Wells

After 35 years of clutter, Jean Wells wanted a simple sewing space in her newly built, eco-friendly home in Sisters, Oregon. She also wanted the space close to the garage to make it easy for her to haul things in and out. Because she chose to line an entire studio wall with picture windows, she had to be creative with storage and work space.

Jean's grandkids can play in the loft while she quilts in her main-level studio. Monorail lighting and cork floors are some of the room's well-planned physical comforts.

"Everything is contained," Jean says of her new studio with well-defined lines. A workstation on wheels has catchall drawers and a flip-up extension to accommodate larger quilt projects. Sliding "design wall" doors are backdrops for fabric play and inspirational photos and magazine pages. A ½-inch gap between the conventional closet doors allows pushpins in the design wall to protrude without getting stuck. Jean also selected cabinets with a comfortable cutting height of 36 inches. An antique divided wood box holds a menagerie of tabletop

tools, and floor-to-ceiling shelves stack fabric by color. "Minimizing clutter frees me to concentrate on my design process," Jean says.

One of the ways she accomplishes the taming of the clutter is by grouping color palettes into wicker baskets, matching fabrics in almost exact proportions to the nature photos and other images she uses as inspiration.

> **Minimizing clutter frees me
> to concentrate on my design process.**
> **—JEAN WELLS**

"I'm constantly working, collecting ideas, and making sketches," Jean says.

To make sliding design doors like Jean's, glue ½-inch-thick cork to hollow-core wood doors. Wrap cork-covered doors with flannel; staple flannel to the back. Mount two tracks an extra ½ inch apart and hang doors.

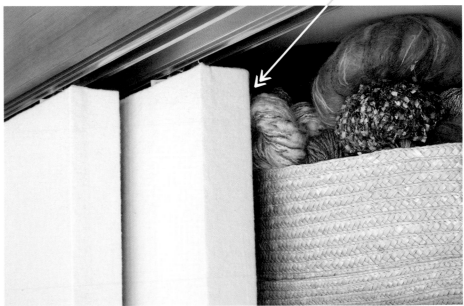

When designing a quilt,
Jean mixes colors and swatches
on her sliding design doors.

Jean stores her in-progress projects on sheet pans on an aluminum baker's rack.

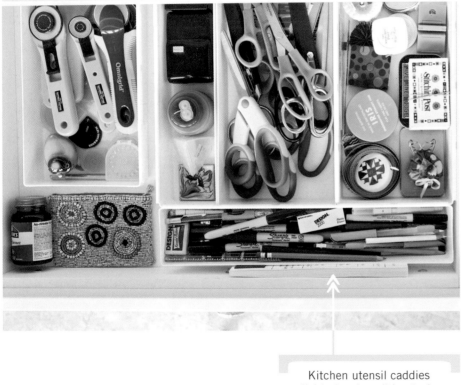

Kitchen utensil caddies divide Jean's quilting tools.

In her journal,
Jean explores the lines
of a rotting tree trunk.

Jean Wells organizes her fabrics
by palette. This group reflects
sagebrush from her yard.

TIPS FOR SETTING UP A STUDIO

✳ Think about what you want to do—sew, scrapbook, knit, or paint—then create your space around it.

creation
STATIONS

Follow the advice of a prolific fabric artist, photographer, and artist to set up your own creative getaway that's family friendly, too. Written by JUDITH STERN FRIEDMAN   Photographed by ADAM ALBRIGHT

A vaulted, naturally lit space above a two-car garage is home to the studio of Valori Wells. High ceilings top areas designated for quilting, designing, painting, developing photos, and even being a parent. "I wanted enough space for my whole family," Valori says. In a custom-made workstation in the center of the room, her daughters can play

The room's dedicated spaces allow Valori Wells to pursue her many creative roles.

with fabrics stored in the drawers below, while above she can dally with quilt designs or work on a computer.

Her drawing table overlooks a canyon behind her home. For additional inspiration she hangs vivid photos and random sketches on fabric-covered cork walls. Custom shelving made of wood precut for stairs fills nooks beneath angled walls, offering easy access to fabric and books. A hand-me-down cutting table, a sewing machine table on wheels, and a drawing table fill the space with what Valori calls "creativity retreats."

Valori Wells

Valori's favorite things hang from a long inspiration wall above the cutting area.

Valori's nature photographs drive her sketches, which evolve into quilt and fabric designs. She's happy now to have her own darkroom.

Family Affair

Valori is able to interact with her family because of the size and layout of her studio. Her daughters have room to play with fabric, stamps, paint, and play at their own art table.

Valori paints her fabric designs while overlooking Squaw Creek Canyon in the beautiful Oregon countryside.

Daughters Olivia and Violette play with fabric scraps and help clean up by putting their scraps into the drawers.

2
Studio Makeovers

Learn how to turn boring and chaotic work spaces into a more organized and inspirational studio with these amazing studio re-dos.

DIY TIP
Boost style and color by decoupaging the fronts of plain bins and magazine files using scrapbooking papers (a pack of paper costs less than $5).

home work

Once a dingy basement, this overhauled home studio is tricked out with organizing ideas you'll want to work out.

Produced by PAMELA S. PORTER   Photographed by GREG SCHEIDEMANN

With a drop ceiling, poor lighting, and old carpet, this walk-out basement was hardly the studio designer Pamela S. Porter envisioned. With a subpar sewing space and a cramped computer station squeezed onto a folding banquet table, Pamela was in desperate need of a more workable space.

In a quest for the perfect studio, the ceiling was the first

To maximize the storage factor without breaking the budget, Pamela used assemble-yourself units from IKEA.

to go, replaced with easy-to-install white planks. Next, Pamela tore out the carpet and two layers of ancient floor tile underneath. After a leveling compound was poured, an engineered hardwood floor—which stands up better to below-grade moisture—was installed.

Recessed lighting and a few drop pendants brighten the work space. Pamela swapped the unsightly folding tables with maple veneered ones. Then came the fun stuff: painting walls spring green and adding softness with curtains, a chair slipcover, and a fun floral-pattern rug.

Before

www.VintageSmith.com

DIY TIP

For a pretty magnet board, cover a piece of galvanized metal with wallpaper and insert into a painted vintage frame.

The painted pegboard wall keeps frequently used items within easy reach, as do the paper-covered soup cans.

Pamela used utilitarian kitchen cabinets for superfunctional storage of tools and supplies.

Since Pamela couldn't find the perfect desk, she made her own by cutting a piece of plywood for the top and covering it with veneer. The desk legs were purchased and screwed to the bottom.

Pullout basket drawers break up the expanse of cabinetry and provide easy access. Look for other pullout options in the home center organization aisle.

With interesting lines, new or old wood brackets add architectural interest while propping up a basic medium-density fiberboard shelf.

With a pretty sitting room adjacent to Margaret's newly overhauled sewing area, the previously dark and dreary space has a fresh, cottage-like feel.

DIY TIP

Paint is a quick and inexpensive way to revive dated brick and grout. An off-white latex in a gloss finish spruces up this fireplace surround.

sew pretty

Before

From friends to family to clients—everybody's talking about Margaret Sindelar's amazing sewing studio makeover.

Produced by PAMELA S. PORTER   Photographed by GREG SCHEIDEMANN

Those who know seamstress Margaret Sindelar know how hard it is for this sentimental woman to let go of anything. Buttons, sewing notions, silk scarves, dishware, flatware, books, and George Washington memorabilia are just some of the collections that fill her home, along with every greeting card she has received over the past 40 years (sorted and labeled by year).

"Mom is definitely a pack rat," says daughter Rachel. "We all want

ABOVE, RIGHT: Before the makeover, Margaret's sewing space was dark and cluttered with piles of buttons, threads, and other sewing notions and had consumed her family's living space.

to send her to Dr. Phil." Instead of a therapist, Margaret and husband Gary welcomed a room makeover. The goal: reclaim the couple's family room turned sewing central while creating an organized, attractive space for Margaret's business.

Once warm and welcoming, the family room had become unrecognizable as Margaret's sewing business expanded over the years. Mismatched cabinets, bolts of fabrics, and scads of sewing notions and equipment had overrun the family space. A makeshift desk was hardly fitting for the night owl, who often sewed into the wee hours of the night by a single-bulb table lamp.

Transforming the gloomy space was critical to the couple's sanity. "We didn't know where to begin," Margaret says. Though they dreaded it, they emptied the room. Only then could they update the canvas—floors and walls—and re-create the room.

"Once everything was out of the room, I was forced to live without all my things for a few months," Margaret says. "That helped me realize I really didn't need it all. So I was very selective in deciding what went back in." Lucky for Gary, he and a new television were both on the list.

For pretty fabric art, roll lengths of fabric and place in a shadow box.

A petite settee had a charming figure, but its solid tan color offered little appeal. For a quick makeover, a quilted twin bedcover (folded and tucked into place) covers the seat and a floral back cushion and a few reproduction accent pillows soften the look.

The new space is all about light—from pretty natural light to the light, airy color palette. The new sparingly dressed bay window was chosen to usher in the sun. Nine recessed lights (where there originally were none) spotlight the room's charm after sunset.

In a range of sizes and pink hues, buttons spell out Margaret's favorite pastime.

DIY TIP

To make this artwork, spell a word or saying using a font from a computer or typography book. Enlarge it to the desired size, cut out, and use a fabrics pencil to trace onto fabric. Fill in with buttons, using fabric glue to secure. Frame when dry.

Opposite the reclaimed family space is Margaret's sewing nook, complete with a generous-size work surface surrounded by cabinetry. A creamy finish keeps the extensive cabinetry from being too heavy, and touches of cherry finishes add unexpected contrast. The desk chair's casters move easily on low-profile carpet tiles.

Before

Magazines are organized in metal bins with easy-make labels cut from magnetic ink-jet paper.

In a rich cherry finish, a sideboard pops off the white paneled wall. The table's drawer shelf extends to create an instant writing desk. In place of an unsightly metal file cabinet, invoices and receipts are kept tidy in blue fabric-covered file boxes.

Make It Yours
Use the storage ideas in your own studio.

❶ PINCUSHION PANACHE
A collection of pincushions looks good enough to eat when covered in sweet vintage fabrics and served up on a pedestal.

❷ IT'S A STICKUP
A bank of 7-inch-deep cabinets allowed for creative storage ideas such as this wallpaper-covered magnetic memo board. We cut a piece of galvanized metal to fit inside and attached it to the cabinet back.

❸ HANG TIME
Inside a cabinet hangs a pegboard sheet that was painted with durable oil-based paint. Furring strips mounted to the cabinet back create a needed gap between the board and cabinet back. A tension rod holds ribbon in place.

❹ EYE CANDY
Margaret's extensive collection of buttons is stored in clear glass jars and displayed on open shelving.

❺ IN THE BANK
Stacks of pretty quilting fabrics are sorted and identified by color using shelf labels. Eighteen spice drawers house notions and supplies.

❻ SMALL BUT MIGHTY
A clever tilt drawer comes to the rescue to reclaim some of the lost storage space underneath the drop-in sewing machine on the countertop.

❼ UTILITY COMPANY
A phone jack and outlet installed inside the cabinet and an outlet in the floor under the desk allow the room to function smartly without unsightly cords.

❽ DIVIDE AND CONQUER
This petite garbage-can insert was easy to retrofit into our small cabinet. Its divided bins are perfect for sorting scraps to discard from those worthy of salvaging for yet another project.

❾ UNDER COVER
Convenient and compact, an ironing board kit is retrofitted into a cabinet drawer, and an outlet is placed into the toe-kick directly below.

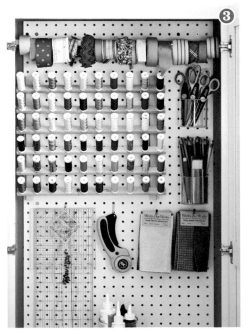

⑤

orange

blue

pink

green

VELCRO RHINESTONES HOOKS & EYES BUTTON KITS

SNAPS TAPE & BRAIDS NEEDLES & PINS PIPING CORD

⑥

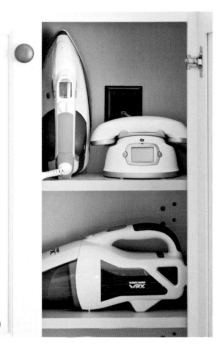

⑦

⑧

⑨

Stephen filled the room with warm tones—sunny yellow on the walls, barn red chairs at the island, and dashes of orange—for an energetic color palette. To mimic sunlight, halogen track lighting shines from above the island. A freestanding work island with storage allows space for spreading out.

creative zone

A boxy suburban basement transforms into a crafts and project room for the entire family.

Designed by STEPHEN SAINT-ONGE   Written by JOANNA SMITH   Photographed by KELLER + KELLER

A bare-bones basement is a blank slate that can be transformed into just about anything. While a space for family entertainment is often a priority, a space dedicated to creativity is a necessity that more and more families are including in their design plans. "It's important to have a space that's not about TV-watching or playing video games, but about using your imagination," designer Stephen Saint-Onge says. With that goal, he used reasonably priced cabinets from a home center to pack storage and function into the corner of an unfinished basement.

Stephen wanted the whole family to use the room, which meant making space for homework, art projects, paying bills, and editing family photos. "I wanted a desk that did it all, but still looked like a piece of furniture," Stephen says. He opted for modular cabinetry that offered drawers, cubbies, and shelving. Stephen ordered his with a distressed white finish to help brighten the windowless room. Butcher block tops both the desk and the island.

Before

Stephen sketched the desk layout, then chose a mix of upper, base, and bookshelf cabinets to maximize storage. Kitchen cabinets left over from a remodel could also be used.

Glues, paints, and other craft supplies are stored in drawers to keep clutter from the desktop. For extra organization, choose dividers to keep supplies corraled neatly.

An all-in-one scanner, printer, fax machine, and copier replaces several separate units and streamlines the desktop.

Inside the closet, small supplies are tamed in containers and pull-out drawers that can be easily picked up and carried to the island workspace.

"This closet is all about storage," Stephen says. Fabric scraps and loose papers land in canvas boxes, but colorful art supplies are on display in clear containers. Adjustable shelving can be reconfigured as needed.

With a fresh coat of paint and new hardware on the old desk, the desk and chair go together seamlessly. The desk was reconfigured alongside two shelving units connected by a wooden surface to take on an L-shape, providing much-needed storage and work space.

fresh accents

A corner workroom filled with hand-me-down furniture and mismatched flea-market finds turns from drab to divine with a few easy updates.

Photographed by WILLIAM HOPKINS, PETER KRUMHARDT, STEVEN MCDONALD, and GREG SCHEIDEMANN
Designed by PAMELA PORTER

Before

D reary. Mismatched. Limiting. All these words describe a previously uninspiring studio that was more of an afterthought than a space to inspire creativity. With its pale blue walls, a collection of furniture cobbled together from

ABOVE RIGHT: With a sliver of usable workspace on the desktop, this small student desk was hardly suitable for creating and computing.

flea markets and garage sales, and even an old computer taking up valuable desktop real estate, it was hard to take the room seriously as a crafting studio. But after a few simple updates, including pretty wallpapered walls, fresh paint to unify the furniture pieces, and newfound spots to store supplies for crafting and gift wrapping, it transformed into a breezy, comfortable space that's a pleasure to spend time in.

Before

A lackluster bulletin board straight from the office supply store begs for a little oomph.

A metal sheet applied over a cork board transforms the board into a magnetic display. The freshly stained frame contrasts beautifully with the newly wallpapered walls, and together with a clipboard decoupaged with decorative paper and a collection of small framed pictures, the grouping makes an attractive addition to the space.

The new desktop extension provides ample area for wrapping gifts and for other projects. The gift-wrap cutter may seem like an indulgence, but it's actually an inexpensive addition to a craft area that keeps rolls of papers, including kraft papers, accessible and easy to cut. Odd-shaped scraps are rolled up and stored in the cubbies of the cupboard hung above the space, and bows and ribbons look pretty in a tiered wire basket.

Rolls of gift wrap and ribbon bows were corraled in a empty wastecan.

Before

3
Get
Organized

Make your ideas and supplies work in a space
that's both functional and inspiring.

idea
centers

Whether it's a collection of paint swatches, scraps of paper, bits of ribbon or a few of your favorite found objects, an inspiration center is an important part of any designer's studio.

OPPOSITE, LEFT: Cinch to Clip
Create an easy-to-access inspiration station from a series of clipboards. For a custom-made look, spray paint the entire board a color that coordinates with your room's decor. Then hang them in neat rows and group your ideas on separate boards or display some of your favorite artwork on each one.

OPPOSITE, RIGHT: Make It Vintage
Dress up a plain-Jane corkboard with neutral fabric and a frame. This cottage-style board displays a collection of vintage ephemera that includes old postcards, tags, sewing needles, and other found objects. Items also hang from clips that are attached to a wire that hangs from the top corners of the frame.

LEFT: Love Your Space
Fit an inspiration board into anyplace you work or have space. A heart-shaped wire photo holder mounted to the center of a bulletin board creates a focal point among a sea of clippings, images, mementos, and swatches. Anything goes in your space—be sure to include anything that will get your creativity flowing.

LEFT: Hit the Spot
A wall dotted with round metal boards not only adds color and a graphic element to a studio space but also provides a handy way to organize inspiring items for individual projects. Use extra-strong tiny magnets to pin up small items without distracting from the grouping of elements, but throw in a couple of larger contrasting magnets to complement the collection.

BELOW: Creativity Squared
A tin ceiling tile works great for displaying lightweight items with magnets. You can purchase new metal tiles at the home-improvement store, or use a salvaged piece. This tile was spray painted white to give it a fresh new finish. The magnets are drawer pulls painted with acrylic paint and backed with extra-strong magnets. Group several tiles together to make an even larger inspiration center.

What Gets Your Creative Juices Flowing?

You never know where your next inspiration will pop up. Here are just a few idea-spurring items you might include in your own creativity center.

* Typography examples
* Beautiful photographs and magazine clippings
* Ribbons and scraps of fabric
* Paint swatches
* Natural textural items such as feathers or dried flowers
* Old game pieces
* Vintage finds such as buttons, postcards, and bits of lace
* Sketches
* Memorabilia

ABOVE: **Stretch Out**
Transform an artist's canvas into an inspiration board with the help of cork and fabric. Start by gluing a piece of cork roll cut to fit the inside of the back of the frame, or cut and piece cork tiles to fit the space. Then cut your fabric at least 3 inches larger than the canvas size on all sizes and stretch the fabric over the frame front, stapling the fabric edges to the wooden stretcher bars on the back.

ABOVE: **Out of the Bottle**
Recycle a collection of leftover corks from wine bottles to make an artistic background for your collection of all things inspiring. Choose a simple, straight-edge frame, then glue the corks to the inside of the backing in an alternating bricklike pattern. Corks are also available online if you don't have a collection of your own.

tools

Finding the right tool when you need it is essential to every designer's studio space. From tiny eyelets and beads to spools of thread, be inspired by these creative ideas.

LEFT: **Shake Things Up**
Keep seed beads, sequins, or buttons in line with a collection of salt and pepper shakers. The perforated tops come in handy for dispensing small bits at a time. Look for interesting shapes and a variety of styles at thrift shops and estate sales.

OPPOSITE: **Wind It Up**
Wrap ribbon and rickrack around vintage textile mill spools, then arrange them inside a pretty tray set on a desktop. By keeping beautiful supplies out in the open, you're more likely to incorporate them into your work.

A Place for Everything

When organizing your design studio, space is almost always at a premium. But rather than fall into the age-old problem of letting your tools overcome your space, utilize these key spots to help maximize your space.

✷ Keep tools and materials at eye level so that you can readily see what you need. Pegboards and shelves are great ways to keep the clutter at bay.

✷ Utilize unused spaces such as backs of doors with over-the-door organizers and small corners of the room with narrow shelving.

✷ Maintain portability of your supplies by using a rolling cart. Roll it underneath your work surface or stow it in a closet when you're not working.

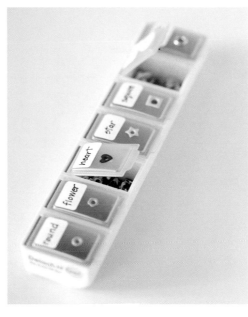

OPPOSITE, TOP: **Measured Success**
Create a custom ruler sorter from scraps of wood. Adjust the cutting depth of a table saw to cut narrow grooves into the wood so that plastic fabric rulers and triangles can sit upright and stay neat and accessible. The stand also works well when backed with a magnet strip so it can be secured to a white board or the side of a metal cabinet.

OPPOSITE, BOTTOM: **Put a Lid on It**
Inexpensive wide-mouth jars are perfect for storing rubber stamps and can be easily pulled off a shelf and brought over to your work area. By separating them by theme into individual jars, you can easily find what you need.

LEFT: **Behind Closed Doors**
With the help of an inexpensive shoe organizer, you can stow hand punches on one side of a door. Slip multiple small ones together in the pouches near the top and the heavier, larger punches in the pouches near the bottom. A clear holder makes everything easy to see.

ABOVE: **Bit by Bit**
Use a small plastic storage box, such as a weekly pill holder, to sort tiny brads, gems, and epoxy accents. Attach one corresponding item to the top of each pop-up lid and add a small label to easily identify the items in each compartment.

paper

Cardmakers, scrapbookers, and craft-a-holics everywhere know that organizing their paper stash can be an overwhelming task. Keep everything neat, tidy, and accessible with these tips.

RIGHT: **Sorted Out**
Store all your scraps in a small bin and create a filing system to organize the bits and pieces by color. Small metal tubs and baskets from the dollar store work well for this task. Divide the contents with trimmed manila file folders to fit your chosen container.

LEFT: Standing Tall
If you prefer vertical paper storage, look for magazine-style paper sorters that can be stowed in a cubby or on a shelf. If using this style of system, it's handy to keep design magazines and inspiring books next to the paper sorters to serve as bookends.

ABOVE: Closet Case
For grab-and-go ease, organize papers in translucent containers and stack them in a hanging sweater unit. Hang the unit from a rod in a closet to stow them out of sight.

BELOW: Cart Smart

Hanging file folders are nothing revolutionary in the office-supply world, but these organizational work-horses aren't limited to filing just receipts and invoices. Hang them from a rolling cart, inside an old metal filing cabinet, or outfit a canvas bin or portable filing box with them and sort your papers according to your needs.

RIGHT: Grab and Go

If your paper collection is extensive, maximize the space in a closet with stackable horizontal storage containers. When dealing with 12×12-inch scrapbook papers, look for containers made specifically for scrapbookers so you can be certain the papers will fit. Sort your papers by color, or by coordinating paper collections, so you can grab a container for your next project and have everything you'll need.

The Paper Chase

Before you jump into organizing your papers, you should decide whether vertical or horizontal storage will work best for your needs. Take a look at the advantages and disadvantages of each:

Vertical Storage

❉ Each sheet is easily accessible

❉ Simple to slide an unwanted sheet back into the sleeve

❉ Papers could bend slightly if rigid sleeves are not used

❉ Works best when stored on adjustable shelving

Horizontal Storage

❉ Papers lie flat so there's no risk of bending

❉ Can be stored in stackable containers or sorting trays

❉ Papers must be sifted through to reach the desired paper near the bottom of the stack

❉ Fits easily into closets

LEFT: **Skirt the Issue**
For compact closet storage, stow papers by subject in 2½-gallon resealable plastic bags (these bags are 14⅜×16 inches, which is room enough to fit thick stacks of paper) and clip them to a multitier skirt hanger. Once you have your papers sorted into the bags, be sure to add a label to the lower corner of each bag for easy identification.

fabric

Big, bulky, and sometimes long yardages make fabric a challenge to store in an efficient and pleasing way. Check out these ideas for bringing sanity to your own stash.

LEFT: Wired and Ready
If your mountains of fabric are begging for some taming, pull-out wire drawers make it easy to access and sort your stash. Group solids and tone-on-tone fabrics by color—you'll appreciate a little bit of organization now when you're hunting for the perfect fabric later.

OPPOSITE, LEFT: In the Fold
Let your favorite fabrics double as decor. This weathered-looking cabinet houses neatly folded yardage that's grouped into color families. The collection looks so appealing, you'll want to keep the doors open all the time for visual inspiration.

OPPOSITE, RIGHT: Get Hooked
Think outside of the box when searching for storage containers. Toss bundles of fabric into an antique wire egg basket and hang it from a hook up high to maximize storage space.

Storage Solutions

Whatever organizational system you choose for your fabric stash, here are some finer tips for storing your favorite fabrics.

✳ When storing stacks of folded fabric, keep the height between the shelves to a minimum. That way, a stack of fabric is manageable to sort through when you pull it out, and you will avoid creating leaning towers of fabric.

✳ Whether you cut specific sizes from every fabric or cut yardages with a project in mind, sorting by cut dimension is a storage option that could help you tame smaller pieces.

✳ Fat quarters fold down to small squares that can be easily organized on open shelving. They're pretty when displayed in a line and are helpful for inspiring color combinations, too.

LEFT: Long and Lovely

If you're limited in the amount of flat storage space you have for your fabric, drape long lengths of fabric or finished quilt tops over hangers to utilize the large vertical space in a closet. This walk-in closet uses both shelf space for smaller scraps and fat quarters and hanging space for long yardages.

ABOVE: Over the Top

Select furniture pieces that can do double-duty as your storage needs evolve. Desk cubbies with a cutting surface on top are perfect for stowing rolled-up quilts in progress or pre-cut fabric bundles ready to be put to use.

4

Small Spaces

Tight on space but need room to work? You don't need an entire room to devote to your craft. All you need is a bit of wall space, an armoire, or a closet to create your own creative workspace.

wall space

Claim a bit of wall and transform it into a space that will get your creative juices flowing.

LEFT: Make a custom work center by attaching counter-height legs to a recycled solid-core door, then giving it a fresh coat of paint. Set a salvaged secondhand store hutch—painted in a contrasting color—on the surface. Gain hanging space by adding hook-friendly pegboard and a magnet-attracting metal panel to the inside of the doors, and make a rolling dolly by attaching casters and bin pulls to medium-density fiberboard (MDF) for storing less frequently used or bulky items underneath the unit.

RIGHT: Every fashionista needs her little creative corner in the world. Copy our compact sewing center by positioning a flirty-legged vanity, comfy chair, and wall-hung cupboard along a wall. The open shelf at the bottom of the cupboard is the perfect size to hold ribbons, patterns, and stacks of fat quarters. Wall sconces light up the space without taking up precious desktop real estate.

If your project command center doubles as a home office, organize it with good-looking steel pegboard. Hang as many panels as you need above a simple desk, then add shelves and bins to hold all of your ribbons, tapes, and other supplies. Look for vibrant colors to brighten up your space.

OPPOSITE: Turn a small writing desk into an out-of-the-way crafts table. A compact desk is a prime choice to put in a small space, such as a spare bedroom, an extra closet, or even the hallway.

ABOVE: A handy tray on top of the desk organizes frequently used art supplies. Vintage milkglass cups and jars make the collection pretty.

ABOVE, RIGHT: Drawers hold crafts supplies to keep the work surface clear.

RIGHT: A rolling cart transformed into an art desk provides plenty of versatility with a durable work surface on top and both open and concealed cubbies below. Use the drop side panel as an extra work surface, tack swatches and sketches to the inside of the door, and stash your fabric scraps, ribbons, and other supplies in the cubbies below.

LEFT: If you don't have the luxury of being able to enclose your workspace, set up a pretty vignette so you don't mind having it on display at all times. Create a vertical storage solution by installing curtain rods across a window or empty stretch of wall space. Then organize color-coordinated ribbons and fabrics for your current project so you can easily find what you need. Use a small table underneath to keep your sewing machine and scissors within reach.

cabinets

Need your own personal space? Trick out an armoire or a cupboard to create a work and storage space to fulfill your creating desires.

LEFT: Utilize every inch of an armoire originally meant for a computer station to make a design-studio-in-a-box. With plenty of work surfaces and drawer and cubby storage inside, it's ideal as a sewing, wrapping, or scrapbooking space. Plug a study lamp in and thread the cord through the opening in the back to help brighten up the space.

OPPOSITE, LEFT: Keep inspirational graphics and to-do lists in sight with clip-style magnets and metal memo boards. Metal sheeting is available in the plumbing aisle of home centers and is easy to cut to size using tin snips. Attach it to the doors with construction adhesive.

OPPOSITE, RIGHT: Outfit drawers with plastic organizers to pigeonhole often-used supplies. Rethink the pullout desktop by storing decorative and wrapping papers in the recess. Pull it out to use it as a wrapping or fabric-cutting counter.

ABOVE: A magnetic strip with canisters attached to the side of the hutch keeps tiny embellishments, such as buttons, eyelets, and brads, standing by. A "work-in-progress" pouch hangs from the hook at the bottom of the strip.

OPPOSITE, RIGHT: This compact storage system is packed with style and function—perfect for a small space. Despite its limited dimensions, this cupboard has open shelves for pretty displays of collections and easy access to often-used items.

ABOVE, LEFT: Painted pegboard is attached to the inside of the cupboard doors with a double layer of mounting tape, but it could be screwed into the wood for added stability.

ABOVE, RIGHT: Rubber stamps are neatly arranged in one of four stacked drawers. Other drawers in this set hold stamp pads, color pencils, punches, and cutting tools.

closets

You might not be able to spare an entire room for your studio but, with a little imagination, an underused closet can become a hardworking space.

NEAR RIGHT: If you're the messy type, this office solution is perfect for you. When you're done working, simply close the doors and your mess disappears.

FAR RIGHT: A typical 6×2-foot closet in today's homes makes a nice hideaway for storing and working on all your projects. With shelving and rods removed, the alcove opens up with possibilities for a counter-height desk, storage cubes, and even a pendant light.

DIY TIP

In a narrow closet such as this 2-foot-wide one, go vertical to maximize storage space. Look for super-functional stacking cubes and drawers to store books, papers, smaller containers, and more.

FAR LEFT: For a punch of color and bonus display and storage, inexpensive fabric covers cork bulletin boards and cardboard boxes, giving the space a coordinating color scheme.

NEAR LEFT: Patterned glass from a stained-glass shop inserts into the bifold closet doors to create a bright, translucent look.

5
Shared
Spaces

If you can't spare a space to devote solely to your craft, transform a room into a dual- or multi-purpose zone with these ideas.

DIY TIP

French doors let light into the office, but can close to hide the mess from guests in the basement crash pad.

work
IT OUT

This basement corner gets crafty with cabinetry and storage tricks. Try these ideas to inspire a fun, functional studio space.

Written by BECKY MOLLENKAMP   Photographed by GREG SCHEIDEMANN   Produced by CATHY KRAMER

K im and Ray Metz needed a space that would do double duty as a home office for Ray and an art studio for Kim. With a growing family, space was at a premium upstairs. The answer? Convert a corner of their basement into a shared work space with the help of stock cabinetry from a home center.

To make their home office as spacious and efficient as possible, they placed their workstations in a U shape, which allowed for ample counter space for both Ray's computer and files and Kim's supplies and projects. Because she likes to stand while crafting, Kim chose tall base cabinets, which allowed for a comfortable standing-height countertop. Slipcovered barstools provide optional seating in three different areas.

When planning the placement of the cabinetry in their basement, the Metzes wanted a unified space that could give each of them a separate work space. By planning intentional gaps in the base cabinetry, turning end units sideways, and extending a portion of the countertop as an island, they were able to maximize storage while creating ample legroom when sitting.

Bright hues inspire Kim, and her favorite palette punches up the basement work area. She coated two walls in a fresh lime green and the other two in orange. To create a focal point on one wall, Kim painted modern flowers in two shades of orange.

DIY TIP

Kim drew the floral designs on a transparency sheet, then used an overhead projector to transfer the shape onto the wall in different sizes. She traced the designs with pencil first and then painted them.

DIY TIP
Kim made newspaper patterns of the back and seat and cut the pieces from blue fabric, then she added hemmed flaps for the seat edges and held the corners together with ribbon ties.

Although they were the right height for the counters, these black-and-purple barstools weren't particularly pretty. Kim gave them a facelift by sewing simple slipcovers. Casters on the bottom of the stool legs allows for easy manueverability around the workspace.

To showcase the room's only window while also diffusing light, Kim created a quick, thrifty solution that's artistic, too. She had a plastics store cut 12-inch squares of plexiglass and drill holes in the top and bottom of each piece. Binder rings connect the squares to each other and to a tension rod across the window top. For color, Kim backed the panels with printed vellum and scrapbook papers.

To maximize storage in the office without breaking her cabinetry budget, Kim lined one wall with three unfinished bookcases, which she painted two shades of vibrant orange. "They were all the same height but it looked a little boring," Kim says. "We built up the middle one about 3 inches with base molding and then pulled it out from the wall to make it stand out." Frosted window film cut into a graphic diamond shape adds dimension to the cabinet doors, and curtains hung from tension rods conceal messes on the bottom shelves.

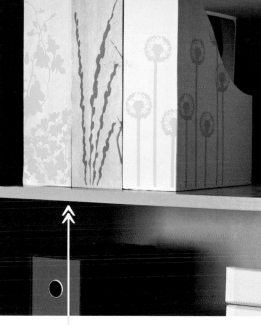

Hanging a few painted dowels on the wall with curtain hardware is a simple way to tame unwieldly rolls of wrapping paper. The entire project cost just a few dollars for dowels and drapery-rod hooks.

Plain white magazine files would be out of place in this colorful office. To continue her palette on the bookshelves, Kim covered basic butlers in a variety of scrapbook papers, including those used in the window treatment.

Originally intended for kitchen use, the stainless-steel system of trays and jars works well for ribbon, scrapbook supplies, and more. "If all of your supplies are hidden, you forget you have them. I like to see what I have to work with," homeowner Kim Metz says.

Pulled away from the wall and outfitted with an extended tabletop, a previously tired buffet makes a spacious surface for spreading out with large projects.

sew VERY happy

Think a multitasking space that accommodates both a DIY work area and space for a guest room is out of reach? Try these savvy solutions that will both inspire your creative side and give visitors the royal treatment.

Written and Designed by PAMELA PORTER   Photographed by KIM CORNELISON

Devoting an entire room to occasional guest visits seems like a waste of space, especially for a DIYer who desperately needs room for her craft. Instead, divide a room into zones for sewing, papercrafting, gift wrapping, computing, and even lounging.

For hardworking rooms like this, every inch has to count. In the crafting corner, the closet is revamped with lots of smart fabric and craft storage, and open shelving elsewhere in the room displays pretty supplies. A dining room buffet with flirty curves is recast as a multifunctional desk. Originally

black, the buffet was treated to fresh green paint, custom wallpaper on the doors, and glass hardware to give it a whole new look. A tabletop made of medium-density fiberboard (MDF) gives plenty of room to showcase fun and functional accessories. A tone-on-tone stenciled wall provides a patterned canvas to accentuate artwork behind the desktop.

By day, the guest area takes on the role of lounge with two chairs and a low drop-leaf table in front of an inconspicuous cabinet. But when guests arrive, the chairs are pushed to the sides of the room, the table rolls

away from the cabinet, and a guest bed folds out from the cabinet to create a dreamy spot for overnight visitors. Cabinets adjacent to the bed offer plenty of storage for bed linens, a coffee maker, and other guest room essentials.

All in all, it's a room filled with touches that creative types and overnight guests both will appreciate.

ABOVE: Maximize your floor space by building a Murphy bed from a kit. Fold it up, and there's ample floor space for projects. Pop it down; it's a landing spot for guests.

RIGHT: There's no need to dedicate an entire closet to guests when the valet bar and bedside cabinets do the trick. Instead, convert the closet into an ultimate storage zone, using off-the-shelf closet components from a home improvement center. The easy-to-assemble units and optional add-on drawers and doors make it a snap to design a storage center. A crisp white finish showcases pretty fabrics, books, and all the fabulous supplies serious crafting addicts seem to collect.

Bifold doors can be restricting, so remove them and use fabric panels that are both attractive and functional. These vibrant purple tie-top panels match the bedding. The panels visually soften the cabinetry and can be drawn to keep closet contents out of visitors' view.

Devote a few low drawers to kids' art supplies so they can put their hands and imaginations to work.

A new generation of powder-coated magnetic steel pegboard is ultra sleek and functional. Choose from standard or custom colors and sizes, then stock up on splendid accessories such as shelves, bins, pegs, and more.

Contain rolls of felt or fabric using this quick and thrifty idea: Cut a fabric measuring tape to size and add a colorful snap.

Old chicken feeders have wiry inserts perfect for holding sorted items. Find them at flea markets and auctions. Add labels with adhesive magnetic paper for categorizing greeting cards.

Pretty supplies, including a paper-lined pencil cup and a kitschy pincushion brighten up the tabletop.

shared spaces 111

When the bed is not in use, its pop-out feet are camouflaged as art plaques with pretty stenciled birds.

Murphy Bed Basics

✳ BUILD

Using basic tools, make a simple box from plywood to fit your twin-, full-, or queen-size mattress. You won't need a box spring. The bed can be positioned horizontally or vertically against the wall, depending on your room's dimensions.

✳ ASSEMBLE

We used the Create-A-Bed kit, *right*, from wallbed.com. At $299, it's a steal compared with most other Murphy bed systems. Detailed instructions and a how-to DVD demonstrate how to use the Create-A-Bed's pivot lift system (no floor mounting required) and ensure the hinge mechanisms are secure.

✳ INSTALL

Attach the Murphy bed to the wall at the studs. Slide your mattress into the box frame, and secure with the straps provided in the kit. The bed should fold up and store securely within its frame.

✳ CUSTOMIZE

The options for personalization are endless. Using a jigsaw, cut a creative headboard from plywood or MDF. You can get imaginative with the design, as long as the headboard is flush with the wall.

If your Murphy bed is flanked by a bank of built-ins or cabinets, consider adding decorative molding on the front of the unit and at the top to keep the grouping cohesive.

You can also install lighting inside or outside the unit (hang a pendant light from the ceiling, like we did, and use a bedside lamp when guests sleep over).

To differentiate the wall behind the bed from its surroundings, we added subtle pattern with a tone-on-tone stencil repeated from another area of the room.

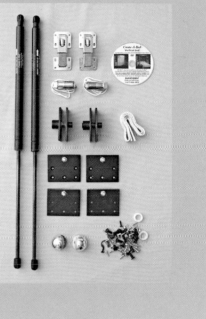

OPPOSITE, LEFT: When the Murphy bed panel pops down, colorful bedding and a hand-cut headboard are revealed inside. A raised panel was even retrofitted in the top drawers so they can serve as bedside tables when pulled out.

OPPOSITE, RIGHT: When the bed tucks away, the majestic hues carry through to a cozy sitting area perfect for reading, knitting, or enjoying a cup of joe. Kids can even gather around to play games or do crafts at the vintage drop-leaf table, which was cut down to coffee-table height and then stenciled.

Bonus rooms, such as this one above a garage, are just that: a "bonus." Because it's not a primary room in the home, the room's shape or size often is determined by the spaces above and beneath it. Ceilings may be sloped underneath the eaves, and the space may be long and narrow because it follows the footprint of the home. To break up the space and make it more workable, this room features a long workstation on one of the side walls.

bonus time

A wasted space over a garage goes to work with the addition of zippy color and pattern, easy DIY built-ins, and super stylish projects that work anywhere in the house.

Designed by ANGIE PACKER and JENI WRIGHT   Photographed by KIM CORNELISON

You know the dilemma: You want to work on your projects, but the kids' "stuff" (that is, things to keep them busy) is inconveniently stowed in another room. So, you set up shop at the kitchen table, making do with substandard working conditions that inevitably lead to a scattering of games, books, and toys across the floor. Not to mention the fact that every time you need something for your project, you have to trek back to your storage area, grab it, and add yet another out-of-place item to your makeshift work area.

Sound familiar? End the cycle by creating a super-stylish, work-friendly room that fits your design needs, while providing space for your family to interact. Perhaps it's a storage room, a spare bedroom, the basement, or even a bonus room over a garage: whatever your space, you'll find that by combining the two functions, you'll supercharge your creativity while maintaining your sanity.

DIY TIP

It looks rich, but wainscoting like this is a doable weekend project. Start by covering the desired wall area with ¼-inch birch plywood (using wood screws), then attach vertical 1×2s every 16 inches. Top the plywood with a 1×6 board adhered flat against the wall, then a cap of 1×2s. Prime and paint.

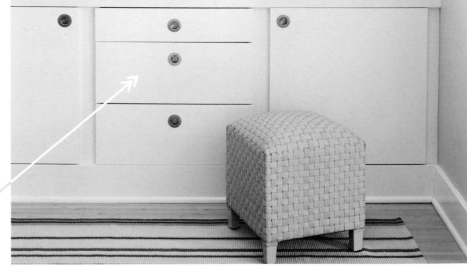

Made from stock kitchen cabinets, this built-in daybed offers loads of storage while providing a cozy spot for kids to read or take a nap. The three units were joined together and to the wall with wood screws, then topped with ¾-inch melamine plywood secured to the cabinets with wood screws. To keep the twin-size mattress from sliding off, the entire built-in unit was topped with a wood box made from poplar 1×4s painted white.

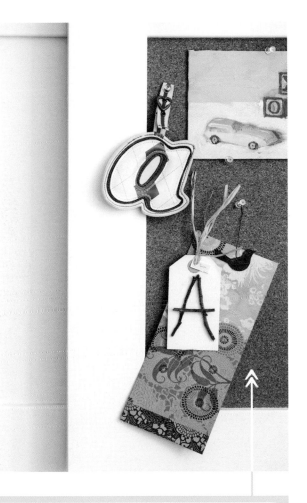

The handy memo center above the desk has a dry-erase board and a sliding corkboard, making it both functional and art-worthy. It's a great place to display kids' artwork along with inspiring ephemera.

To custom fit a desk in the long spaces beside a corner window while staying on a budget, IKEA table legs and a stock kitchen cabinet allow for two people to sit and work at the same time. The top is stained birch plywood, and edged with dimensional lumber, but a hollow-core door would also work.

DIY TIP

When hanging a small grouping of pictures, trace your art on kraft paper or newspaper, cut it out, and tape it to your walls to perfect the arrangement. Hang the top piece just above eye level, then work your way down. When you're happy with the grouping, hang the art from picture hooks.

When planning your space, position a chair by the window to take advantage of the light and the view.

Take It Home

If you're short on time (and budget), try this entry-level project using ready-to-assemble shelves from IKEA, plus stock moldings, boards, and high-gloss paint from a home store.

❋ **START WITH THE SHELVES**

Basic Expedit bookcases are placed horizontally to create a low series of shelves, but they can be used vertically for height interest (great for basements or living spaces that need a focal point boost).

❋ **BUILD UP A BASE**

Create a foundation for the shelves by building a box the length and width of the shelves from poplar 1×6s. Cut with a table saw or jigsaw, and screw together the pieces using a drill. Position the first bookcase above the box, then anchor the shelves using wall fasteners. Repeat with the remaining bookcases. Screw the bookshelves together with long wood screws to secure the units.

❋ **FINISH IT**

Cut 1×6 boards and shoe molding to edge the base. Use a miter box and saw to cut 45-degree angles for the corners. Pin-nail or glue in place. For the top of the shelves, cut a board to the width and depth of the base molding, then secure to the shelves with heavy-duty adhesive, such as Gorilla Glue; clamp. Finish the top by priming, then painting the top a high-gloss white (use two coats).

The wall adjacent to the workstation features a bank of low bookshelves to hold kid stuff. The low profile ensures that the shelves won't topple, which is the safest bet when small children are around. Plus, the top of the shelves makes a great display area for bigger items, along with a perfect spot for a TV and DVD player. Small, easy-to-lose toys can be tucked away inside the baskets and bins in the cubbies.

DIY TIP
Make your own low-cost artwork by drawing a shape, such as this stylized tree, onto plywood and cutting it out with a jigsaw. The natural, unfinished wood adds to the organic look.

Configured to accommodate multiple workers with a computer station and a movable desk, this studio offers something for everyone in the family.

family-friendly WORKSPACE

By combining flexible storage for computing, crafting, doing homework, and more, this space works as hard as it plays. Get to know these must-have elements.

Field editor LINDA HUMPHREY   Photographed by JOHN GRANEN

ere's the dilemma: You need space to do your scrapbooking and gift wrapping. The kids need a place to do homework. And you and your spouse need a spot to pay bills and surf the Internet. How do you combine all these functions when a tiny extra bedroom is all you can spare?

Read on for innovative ways to make the most of a small space that's fit for everyone in the family.

Corkboard provides space for a calendar, while a magnetic dry-erase board lets family members brainstorm or leave notes.

Multiple drawers under a central work island give each family member a place for essential tools, project materials, and books.

Tension curtain rods and adjustable shelves transform an open bookcase into a crafts and gift-wrapping station where everything is easy to access.

More Essentials for a Family Workroom

Working together in one space can be fun when you design the room with function in mind.

✱ Movable work surfaces, such as the steel-topped table on casters shown on *page 120,* can accommodate one or several workers.

✱ Cabinets with open storage, movable shelves, and predrilled holes for cords adjust to fit changing technology.

✱ Matching office supplies, such as a collection of basic white boxes and binders, can support a variety of projects and can be supplemented or replaced as needed.

✱ Comfortable, durable flooring makes a work space inviting and easy to clean. Here, individual pieces of carpet tile can be swapped out depending on wear.

Outfitting a closet with floor-to-ceiling shelves and drawer units keeps in-progress projects and less frequently used resources out of sight.

A high cubby, made by modifying a standard kitchen cabinet, gives the washer and dryer in this studio/laundry room a built-in look, while the shelves and a counter-height desk provides a writing area and a space for a computer.

awash in style

Put a new spin on the laundry room by creating a smart space that goes one (or two) better—think crafting, gift wrapping, even potting plants. Designed by JOHN LOECKE   Photographed by KIM CORNELISON   Written by SARAH STEBBINS

Say the words "basement" and "laundry room" in the same sentence and your imagination almost immediately conjures up a dark, dreary, work space. And that's exactly what designer John Loecke faced when he was recently confronted with a messy basement corner complete with an outmoded washer and dryer from the 1980s, a makeshift shelving unit piled high with ugly plastic totes, and an old kitchen table with mismatched chairs serving as a gift-wrapping and crafts project center. Although the space served many functions, it was highly inefficient when it came to user-friendliness.

That's when John came up with a plan to re-do the space into a more welcoming and streamlined room.

First, he brightened the basement with sky blue paint on the walls, crown molding near the ceiling, and heavy-duty paint on the concrete floors. Next, he swapped out the outdated washer and dryer with a pair of stacking, high-efficiency models, and housed them inside a built-in cabinet that he constructed in conjunction with a standing-height desk and shelves. The old utility sink was replaced with dual wash basins, creating a hand-laundering and potting station in one.

Even though the space is small, everything has a place. Read on for more ideas for putting essential items within reach, maintaining a clutter-free workspace, and making environmentally responsible choices in your room design—all while carving out a multipurpose space.

Formerly a cluttered basement bogged down with piles of containers and unkempt craft supplies, this space exudes function and style. Hooks on the pegboard are used for keeping paintbrushes, scissors, and other tools tidy, while cubbies above the countertop store fabric and snapshots in opaque containers and decoupaged metal bins. Glass jars make it easier to find items like beads and buttons. Rolls of wrapping paper fit perfectly in a wine rack wedged between the lower cabinets.

The Corian countertop, a durable surface made from acrylic and natural stone, is ideal because you can buff out scratches with a nylon scouring pad.

Kitchen cabinets installed along one wall give the workspace a finished look while providing space to tuck things out of sight.

DIY TIP

Choose inexpensive, off-the-rack cabinets in standard sizes to fit your room's dimensions.

John furnished the room with rehabbed pieces, like this flea market library table. He cut a couple of inches off the legs, attached casters, and stained the bottom a blue-gray. Secondhand chairs got a fresh coat of paint and splashy new cushions.

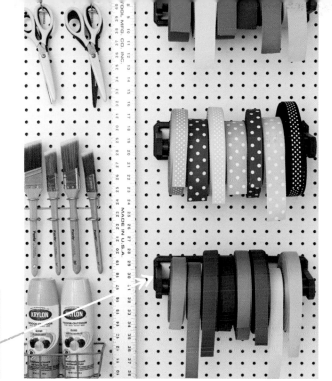

John transformed a paper towel holder into a ribbon dispenser. A screwdriver rack holds paintbrushes.

Basic canvas storage boxes can be personalized with ribbon, cloth, and adhesive scrapbooking letters.

A pull-out spice cabinet is great for small supplies like paints, glitter, and glue.

A pair of built-in garbage and recycling bins hold bulky items like yarn and rolls of fabric.

Decorate binders with scraps of different ribbon as an organizing trick: Put seed catalogs in a polka-dot holder, owner's manuals in a striped one, and so on.

A bulletin board cut from Homasote (a building material also available at home stores), placed above the desk and painted to match the walls blends right in.

DIY TIP

Get a similar look by mounting a countertop on basic base cabinets or table legs, which are available unfinished at hardware and home stores.

Pull up a painted flea market seat and play around with unexpected containers, such as vases, to corral supplies.

John used cabinet shelving and legs designed for an island to create this custom desk.

The Green Touch

How to pull off an environmentally responsible (and money-saving) redo. Choose cabinets, countertops, and paint made by companies that pledge to use adhesives and finishes containing low levels of pollutants, known as VOCs, and, if applicable, follow sustainable forestry practices. Check for a certification from the Kitchen Cabinet Manufacturers Association's Environmental Stewardship Program, the Greenguard Environmental Institute, the Forest Stewardship Council, or, in the case of paint, a label that reads "zero VOCs."

✳ BRIGHT IDEA

Replace traditional incandescent bulbs with compact fluorescents (CFLs), which use 75 percent less energy and last up to 10 times longer. The new generation of CFLs come in a wide array of shapes (not just spirals), including the recessed spotlights installed in this room. For more information on how to get the best bulb for the job, visit energystar.gov.

✳ UPGRADE APPLIANCES

If your washer and dryer are more than 10 years old, consider replacing them with energy-efficient front-loading models or redesigned top-loading ones. Those with the Energy Star label use about half as much water as older machines, saving up to $145 a year on utility bills.

DIY TIP

If you can't find a stand, use a low table and cut holes in the top for pipes. Install a shelf or cabinet overhead for vases and gardening supplies. You can still set up a potting area even if your room doesn't have plumbing—just keep an extra-large watering can handy.

Like many laundry rooms, this one already had a sink. But John felt dual basins would be more versatile for tasks like hand-washing clothes, potting plants, and flower arranging. He had a plumber install new faucets and retrofit a vintage metal wash stand with drains to hold two large galvanized tubs.

6
Project Ideas

Conquer the clutter and bring order to your supplies with these can-do ideas for sprucing up your space.

take a message

An aluminum cookie pan—sans the dough—makes an excellent backing for ephemera and messages posted with decorative magnets.

MATERIALS
Cookie sheet
Decorative paper
Pencil and scissors
Spray adhesive or double-stick tape
Clear, flat-bottom florist's stones
Magnet disks

1 With the patterned paper facing up, place the cookie sheet face-up on top of the paper. Using a pencil, trace around the bottom of the pan onto the paper. Remove the pan, then trace another line aproximately ½" inside the first line; cut along this line, rounding the corners.

2 Use spray adhesive or double-stick tape to attach the patterned paper to the inside of the pan.

3 Make a set of coordinating magnets by backing flat-bottom florist's stones with colorful papers and glued-on magnets.

Sort It Out

Find a drawer adjacent to your work space and use drawer dividers to keep each tool in its spot.

give an inch

Old advertising rulers can be found for cents at flea markets. Turn them into photo mats worthy of display in a studio space by using a handsaw to miter the corners and then join them with wood glue.

MATERIALS
Narrow-edge picture frame
Miter saw
Fine-tooth handsaw
Wood glue
Heavy-duty stapler (optional)

1 Measure each side of the frame.

2 Using a miter saw and a fine-tooth handsaw, cut the ruler into four pieces to fit the frame sides. Plan the cuts at 45-degree angles, making sure to cut the ends at opposing angles to get a proper fit when joining the pieces.

3 Join the rulers together with wood glue at the joints. For extra durability, use a heavy-duty stapler to place a staple at each seam.

4 Insert the ruler mat into the picture frame and place a photo behind the mat. Replace the picture frame backing to hold the pieces in place.

get it in the bag

Instead of using standard bookends, sew "sandbags" from fun, colorful fabric to corral your books, files, and folders.

MATERIALS
2 fabric scraps at least 8×10" each
Plastic resealable bag
Sand

1 Cut two 8×10" pieces of fabric for each sandbag.

2 Place the fabric pieces with right sides together, and sew three sides using ½" seam allowances. Turn right side out.

3 Fill a plastic resealable bag with sand. Insert the bag through the opening in fabric. Topstitch around all sides to finish.

Jar Stars

A collection of thrift-store jars makes an eclectic and attractive way to display ribbons, buttons, and other supplies. Group your supplies by color, size, or shape—whatever suits your needs.

Recycled Storage

Don't throw away all your empty potato chip and coffee cans. Wrap them in pretty paper and use them to store small crafting items, such as buttons, pins and needles, bobbins, and embellishments.

Magnet Mania

Round up a few scraps and spare magnets to make all of these attractive baubles
for $5 or less. Try adhering papers, attaching felt embellishments, and layering buttons
onto clear marbles and magnet backs to make them. For a firm hold, secure the magnets
to the items with a heavy-duty adhesive, such as E6000, Krazy Glue, or Liquid Nails.

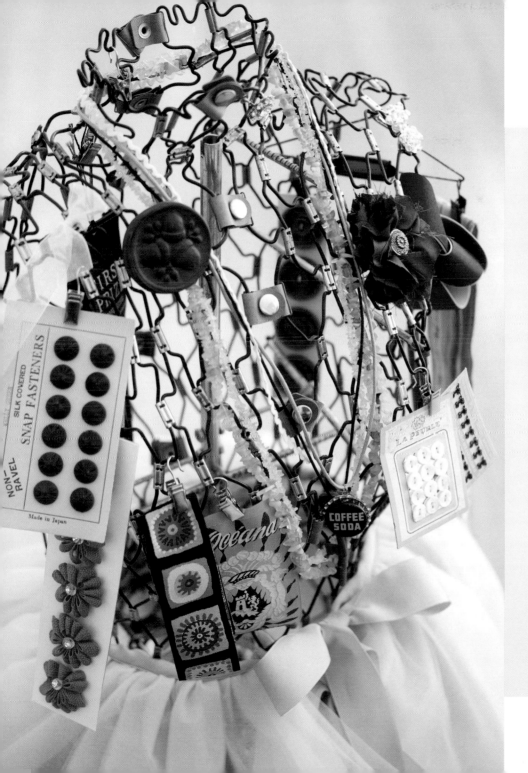

Style Maker

Play dress-up with a vintage wire dress form by clipping on button cards, ribbons, and old jewelry, and dangling fun necklaces over top. Many of the items hang with pinch-style clips attached to a wire hook. A flirty tulle skirt tied around the waist adds a fun touch.

Book Nook

A shelf isn't the only solution to storing books. Slip them between the spindles of a wall-hung plate rack for an interesting display idea. Place a favorite book or a larger hardcover on a cookbook stand on top of the rack.

close the case

Give your laptop some serious personality with a cute sleeve made from a single tea towel.

MATERIALS

Tea towel
Laptop computer
Scissors and straight pins
Sewing machine

1 Unfold the towel, then center the laptop computer on it. For the sides, cut the tea towel so it's 2 inches wider than your laptop. Press sides under ½", repeat, then sew a ½" hem.

2 Use scraps to make ties. For each tie, cut two 8×2" strips, place right sides together, and sew ½" hems along the two long sides and one short side. Clip the corners, turn right side out, press, and topstitch the edges.

3 Pin two strips to one short side of the towel 4" from the outside edges; sew. Fold the sleeve over the laptop, then determine the best placement of the matching ties. Fold under the raw edges of the ties, and sew in place.

Ready to Wrap

Pull-out drawers underneath a countertop are
handy for keeping rolls of wrapping paper tidy.
Keep ribbons and some card-making supplies,
such as rubber stamps, papers, and paints, stored
in cabinet-door-mounted wire racks.

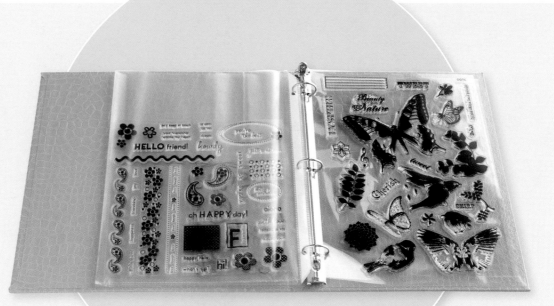

Pretty Pin-Ups

A pair of small corkboards provides a pretty place to
hang scrapbook-ready mementos, crafts to-do ideas, or
supply lists. Stack three cake stands for tiered crafts
storage. Anything you get off the counter instantly
expands your available work surface.

Stamp and Store

If you're a stamper, taming stamps can be a challenge.
Keep acrylic stamp sheets tidy by punching holes in them or
slide them into page protectors and store them in binders.

break time organization

Even a grungy old lunch box can shine again with a little TLC. With a Thermos bottle tucked inside, this one offers plenty of solutions for storing art supplies.

MATERIALS
Salvaged lunch box and Thermos bottle
Spray primer
Spray paint
Painter's tape
Self-adhesive shelf paper

1 Prime and spray-paint the lunch box inside and out. Repeat with the Thermos lid, masking off the screw band with painter's tape.

2 Measure and trim the self-adhesive shelf paper to cover the inside of the lunch box; press to apply.

3 Measure and trim the self-adhesive shelf paper to fit around the outside of the Thermos bottle.

4 Store long-handled paintbrushes in the Thermos, short pencils in the lid, and larger art supplies inside the box.

Hang It Up

A shallow hanging cupboard provides plenty of storage for small items, such as craft supplies. Hang one cupboard, or a pair, wherever more put-away space is needed. Add finials to the top to corral wrapping paper and thread spools of ribbon onto a tension rod beneath the cupboarrd.

Wash, Dry, and Craft

A crafts station can be hung on any wall in the house, even above
a washer and dryer. Open shelves accommodate oddly shaped supplies,
such as a sticker maker and floral arrangement containers. Small drawers
hold notions, embellishments, and small tools while keeping
the space uncluttered.

Take It with You

Make your crafts projects go more smoothly
by organizing everything in a durable toolbox.
With multiple trays, it will keep things handy
and portable.

topper show stopper

Sheets of gutter topper and a few clothespins transform a boring wall into a modern display for your creative inspiration.

MATERIALS

Mesh gutter topper (we used 9 pieces)
Metal cup hooks
White spray paint
Clothespins
Magnets
Tacky glue
Inspirational items to hang

1 Measure the short side of one gutter topper to determine where to place the hanging hooks. Drill two small holes in the wall, then manually screw the hooks into the wall.

2 Repeat Step 1 for each gutter topper. Hang them at different heights as shown.

3 Spray paint the clothespins your desired color—we chose white to let the artsy cards stand out. Let dry.

4 Glue a small magnet to the back of each clothespin. You don't need much glue—a small dot will do.

5 Hang paint swatches, cards, or any other inspirational object on the display.

Organize with a Wine Rack

An under-the-shelf wine and stemware rack blends style and function and utilizes otherwise overlooked space. Glass cylinders hold pencils, markers, pens, and brushes, while ink pads can be stashed on the stemware rack.

In the Cards

Here's a fresh idea for a leftover mint container. Cover both the outside and inside of the lid with decorative paper and place your business cards inside. Use another embellished container for cards you receive.

Bin There

Check out the antiques store or flea market for character-rich items you can use for storage. Here, an old lunch pail goes to work storing CDs (it's lined with felt to keep scratches at bay).

enliven a lamp

Instead of a standard task lamp, go bold with a quick facelift project.

MATERIALS

Salvaged lamp
Spray paint in desired color
Veneer sheets
Stencil
White paint
Sponge pounce brush

1. In a well-ventilated area, paint the base of an old lamp with spray paint. Allow the paint to dry.

2. Using the old shade as a pattern, cut thin veneer pieces the height of the shade and glue them around the shade.

3. Stencil a pattern around the base of the veneer with white paint.

Divide and Conquer

A plate rack with vertical dividers, a shelf, and a row of hooks provides flexibility for storing scrapbook paper, stickers, photo files, completed pages, unfinished work, and other inspirations. Use the dividers to file magazines, folders, and notepads, too. Label each divider so items are easy to find and to put away. Store tags, paper clips, and embellishments in pretty bowls on the shelf. Slip markers and scissors into hanging metal pails.

Spice Is Nice

Turn round magnetic storage tins meant for spice storage into a wall-mounted caddy for small embellishments. Screw the metal backing to the wall and arrange the tins in rows to keep your supplies visible but out of the way.

clip it together

Paint stripes in several colors to enliven a plain clipboard.

MATERIALS

Clipboard
Painter's tape
Acrylic paint in assorted colors
Foam paintbrushes

1 Position painter's tape across the width of the board, spacing the tape as desired.

2 Paint the areas between the tape using different colors for each stripe; remove the tape and let dry.

3 Position painter's tape to mask off remaining unpainted areas. Paint the remaining stripes, remove the tape, and let dry.

4 Embellish stripes as desired (as the top stripe was done on this example). Use stickers, or paint small motifs, if desired.

Tote-ally Personal

Give a plain-Jane canvas tote a high-impact makeover with punched paper flowers, ribbon, pom-pom fringe, and rickrack. To create the leaves, fold ribbon scraps in half, staple the ends together, and tuck them behind the stem. Attach the pieces to the tote with needle and thread, or with adhesive or brads.

round and round

Craft an inexpensive spinning tool caddy for your desktop using recycled jars and cans.

MATERIALS

Wooden lazy Susan (can be found at kitchen supply stores)
A variety of clean cans and jars with labels removed
Medium- and fine-grit sandpaper
Acrylic paint and sponge brush
Clear sealant
Masking tape
Patterned papers

1 Use medium- and then fine-grit sandpaper to sand the surfaces of the lazy Susan. Remove the sanding dust. Paint the lazy Susan with acrylic paint using a sponge brush; let dry.

2 Brush clear sealant over the painted surface; let dry.

3 Cover any sharp can edges with masking tape. Cut patterned paper to fit the sides of the cans.

4 Use spray adhesive to attach the paper to the can sides. Add ribbon to cans and jars if desired.

5 For a more permanent fixture, use a heavy-duty adhesive to attach the bottoms of the cans and jars to the lazy Susan.

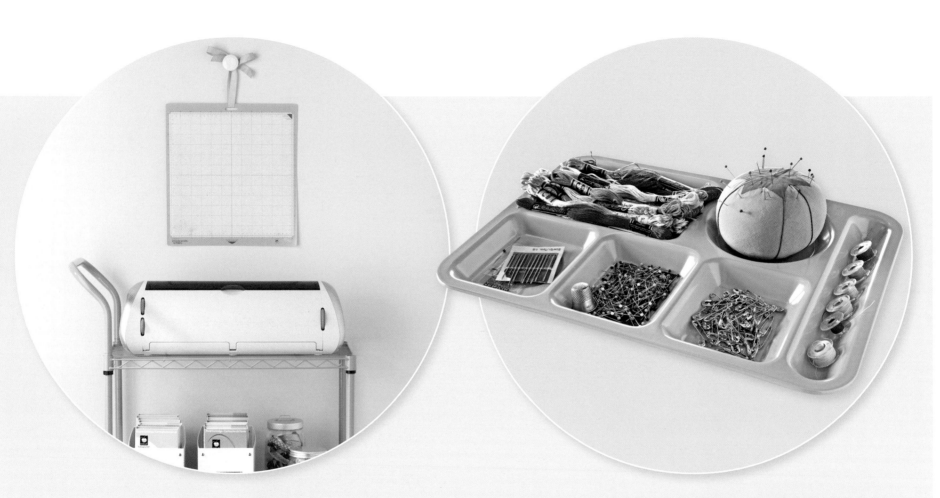

Cut-Up Clues

If your die-cutting tool includes a mat, thread a ribbon through the top and hang it from a decorative hook above the die-cutting tool. Store the tool on top of a rolling cabinet or cart and keep the accessories below. Stash dies or cartridges in baskets or binders with divided page protectors to hold each die or cartridge.

Tray Bien

Try using a school-lunch-inspired trick to keep your pins and needles (and other crafting supplies) in place. Use different compartments in a cafeteria-inspired divided tray to organize needles, pins, embroidery thread, and bobbins. The round compartment is perfect for a pincushion or rolled measuring tape. Look online or in thrift stores for trays.

sign of the times

Make your sign of the times using random new and old numbers, a round cake pan, and a clock mechanism.

MATERIALS

Round cake pan
Battery-operated clock mechanism
Drill
Heavy-duty adhesive suitable for metal
Random found numbers in a variety of
    sizes (typesetter blocks, house
    numbers, blocks, etc.)

1 Drill a small hole through the center of the cake pan.

2 Insert the clock mechanism through the inside of the pan so the battery is inside the pan and the clock hands are on the back of the pan.

3 Position the numbers around the edge of the back of the pan, gluing them in place as you layer pieces.

To the Letter

Inexpensive desk organizers get dressed to impress in brown, blue, and green felt letter stickers and accents. If your plastic organizer doesn't match your color scheme, spray-paint it. (To save on sanding time, select a formula made for plastics.) After the paint dries, randomly cover the surface with adhesive letters and symbols.

Mobile Crafts Cart

Retrofit an old end table into a cart that can function as a mobile crafting station. File papers, stickers, and scrapbook pages below, and stash tools and markers on top. Push it wherever you want for an instant work space.

On a Roll

Straw dispensers from the dollar store rise to the occasion to hold towers of ribbon spools. Remove the top of the dispenser inserts and slide the ribbons onto the rods. Not only are unruly ribbons kept in check, but they make pretty displays as well.

bin-tin-tin

Keep odds and ends in this three-tier stand instead of in a junk drawer.

MATERIALS

Three vintage tins in graduated sizes
Threaded rod
Copper pipe
Nuts
Washers
Plywood
Drill with assorted bits
Pipe cutter
Jigsaw
Hacksaw
Metal file
Compass

1 Cut a circular piece of plywood to fit inside the lid of the largest tin.

2 Using a compass, find the center of each tin, the lid, and the plywood piece. Drill holes into the centers of all of the pieces.

3 Put the plywood into the tin lid and place it onto the threaded rod, securing it with a washer and bolt on the bottom to create the base.

4 Thread on a bolt a few inches up from the base and add the largest tin. Repeat for the two other tins.

5 Adjust the heights of the tins and mark the height of the threaded rod inside the top tin. Add ¾ inch to this measurement to accommodate a washer and nut.

6 Measure the distances between the tins to accommodate the copper pipe. Using a pipe cutter, cut the copper pipe into sections using the measurements above. Cut the threaded rod with a hacksaw. File any sharp edges.

7 Disassemble the stand and reassemble, placing the copper pipe between sections.

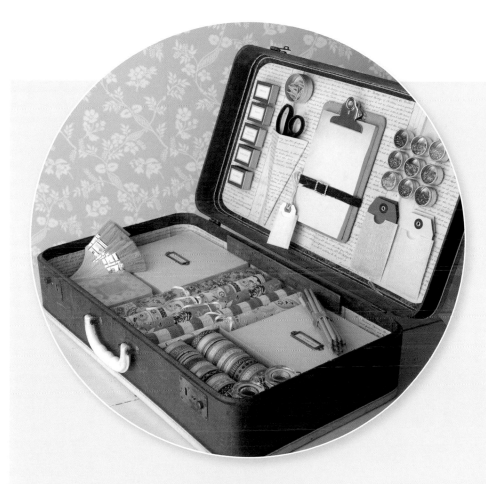

Get a Handle on It

Small luggage pieces become fun when used as crafts storage and can easily be tucked away when not in use. Glue a metal sheet to the inside of the lid and attach magnetic spice jars to store embellishments. In addition, suitcases can hold unfinished crafts projects and scrapbook-ready photos.

Tower Trick

Create a desktop organizer by covering quart paint cans with scrapbooking paper. Use double-stick tape under the edges to secure the paper. To make a display, stack the cans and glue them together. Use the same idea with gallon cans to store larger items.

Help Yourself

Purchased cereal dispensers mounted on the wall make a much more interactive—and fun—way to display and dispense buttons.

frame it up

Save a frame and a baking rack from curbside demise
to make a hardworking magnet board.

MATERIALS
Picture frame with wide molding
Spray paint
Salvaged wire oven rack or wire
    mesh from the hardware store
    (test the conductivity with a
    magnet before selecting)

1 Brush off any loose paint on the
picture frame with a stiff wire
brush. Sand any rough areas
with medium-grit sandpaper.

2 Spray paint the picture frame
molding in a well-ventilated
area.

3 Use wire cutters to cut the wire
sheet so that it is slightly larger
than the picture frame opening.

4 Using a heavy-duty stapler or
tacks, attach the wire sheet to
the edges on the back of the
opening of the frame.

Ready to Roll

Adapt a rolling metal shelf unit with locking
casters into a movable cutting table for quilting and
sewing projects by adding a flat surface to the top
for cutting. Underneath the cutting table, keep
unfinished projects—and the supplies needed to
finish them—on the shelves.

Hidden Potential

Don't have a dedicated crafts room? No problem. Plastic storage boxes keep supplies organized in any temporary work space and are easy to hide under the bed, sofa, or entertainment center.

Make an Index

Instead of a solid desk drawer, vintage metal card-catalog holders are perfect storage for office papers.

create some shade

This tall lampshade gets a quick pick-me-up with a tea towel.

MATERIALS
Lamp with straight-sided shade
Tea towel
Scissors
Spray adhesive
Hot-glue gun and adhesive

1 Wrap the tea towel around the shade and cut off the excess length and width, keeping one finished side and the finished bottom.

2 Spray adhesive onto the wrong side of the towel and wrap the fabric around the shade, smoothing out air bubbles by hand.

3 To finish, overlap the raw edge with the finished seam and tack it down with hot glue. If desired, mask any visible raw edges by gluing on a piece of ribbon or trim.

The Great Divide

Dedicate a dresser in a back closet to your artistic side. Metal label holders make it clear what each drawer holds, and they may stop you from randomly throwing in supplies and creating another mess. Dividers bring order to the goodies inside.

mouse mat

A plain cork tile transforms into a one-of-a-kind mouse pad with some careful cutting and paint.

MATERIALS
Cork tile
Frame stamp and ink
Plain paper
Laser-cut paper
Acrylic paint and sponge brush
Clear protective spray

1 Stamp a frame image onto paper with ink. Enlarge the stamped image with a photocopier to the desired size. Cut around the outside edge of the frame with scissors to make a template.

2 Lay the template on the cork tile and trace around it with pencil. Remove the template, and then using a crafts knife held at a 45-degree angle, make a beveled edge as you cut the frame out along the lines.

3 Cut laser paper to fit inside the frame. Layer the paper over the cork for a mask. Use a foam brush to paint over the mask; carefully lift the mask before the paint dries to reveal the pattern. Outline the frame with a line of paint to define the edges. Let the paint dry.

4 Spray the entire surface with protective sealant.

Recipe for Success
Organize buttons, pins, and other sewing clutter in a salvaged muffin tin and place it on your desktop. Place a pincushion in one of the circular openings to keep pins close at hand.

Glass with Class
Hit the aisles of a home improvement center and pick up replacement covers for outdoor sconces. Turn them into sturdy desktop containers to hold pens, pencils, and paintbrushes. The wide bases minimize tipping, and the grooved sides add fun detail.

Hole in One
Unwind yarn or curling ribbon with ease by threading the end through the hole of a sugar dispenser and placing the ball inside the jar.

Put a Spin on It

A rotating spice rack is perfect for safely storing small embellishments like buttons, brads, and beads.

Tool Time

If you find yourself turning to a few chosen tools time and time again, set yourself up with a handy wall organizer to keep your most often used items close at hand. This organizer has pockets for scissors and pens—which also fit styluses and burnishers—along with space for inspirational tidbits and papers.

Castoff for Cards

A castoff cassette tape case gets a new lease on life as a handy holder for business cards. To get the look, measure and trim cardstock to fit the plastic case's back and lip and decorate with flowers and gems, or size digital canvases and embellishments found with scrapbooking software to fit the case, and print out the designs on photo paper.

workbook

Use the paper on the following pages to note your
favorite ideas and plan the layout of your studio.

KEY: ¼ inch = 1 foot

**It's not about being perfect,
but enjoying what you do.
Set aside time to be creative.**
—ROBYN PANDOLPH,
QUILT DESIGNER